DATE DUE

JUN 20 03			
JUN 2 2 2017			
GAYLORD			PRINTED IN U.S.A.

ULTRAMARINE

Books by Raymond Carver

FICTION

Where I'm Calling From
Will You Please Be Quiet, Please?
Furious Seasons
What We Talk About When We Talk About Love
Cathedral

POETRY

A New Path to the Waterfall
Winter Insomnia
At Night the Salmon Move
Where Water Comes Together with Other Water
Ultramarine

PROSE AND POETRY

No Heroics, Please
Fires

VINTAGE BOOKS
A DIVISION OF RANDOM HOUSE
NEW YORK

RAYMOND CARVER

ULTRAMARINE

FIRST VINTAGE BOOKS EDITION, OCTOBER 1987

All rights reserved under International and Pan-American
Copyright Conventions. Published in the United States
by Random House, Inc., New York, and simultaneously in
Canada by Random House of Canada Limited, Toronto.
Originally published, in hardcover, by Random House, Inc., in 1986.

Library of Congress Cataloging-in-Publication Data
Carver, Raymond.
 Ultramarine.
 I. Title.
[PS3553.A7894U58 1987] 811'.54   87-40081
ISBN 0-394-75535-9 (pbk.)

Acknowledgment is gratefully given to the following magazines, in which some of the
poems in this book originally appeared:

The Atlantic: "Sinew"; *Crazyhorse:* "Bonnard's Nudes," "The Young Fire Eaters of
Mexico City"; *The New Yorker:* "Kafka's Watch," "Cutlery"; *Northwest Review:* "The
Phone Booth," "What I Can Do," "Powder-Monkey," "From the East, Light,"
"Egress," "Limits," "Asia'; *The Ohio Review:* "Simple," "The Projectile"; *The
Ontario Review:* "The Autopsy Room," "Its Course," "Migration"; *The Paris Review:*
"Hope," "Sleeping"; *Poetry:* "Shiftless," "The Sensitive Girl," "Balsa Wood," "The
Rest," "Mother," "Mesopotamia," "Stupid," "A Tall Order," "The River"; *Plough-
shares:* "An Afternoon," "Cadillacs and Poetry," "This Morning," "Union Street: San
Francisco, Summer 1975," "Vigil"; *Scripsi* (Australia): "The Window," "Evening,"
"The Phenomenon," "Scale," "The Meadow," "Heels," "The Schooldesk"; *Seneca
Review:* "The White Field," "Where the Groceries Went," "The Gift"; *Tendril:* "The
Garden," "In the Lobby of the Hotel del Mayo"; *TriQuarterly:* "Sweet Light," "The
Mail"; *Zyzzyva:* "The Pen."

Other poems appeared in limited editions published by William B. Ewert.

Manufactured in the United States of America
B987654321

DESIGNED BY BARBARA M. BACHMAN

TESS GALLAGHER

Sick with exile, they yearn homeward now, their eyes
Turned to the ultramarine, first-star-pierced dark
Reflected on the dark, incoming waves.

——D E R E K   M A H O N , ''Mt. Gabriel,'' from
Antarctica, 1985 (The Gallery Press)

Contents

One

This Morning   3
What You Need for Painting   5
An Afternoon   6
Circulation   7
The Cobweb   9
Balsa Wood   10
The Projectile   11
The Mail   13
The Autopsy Room   15
Where They'd Lived   17
Memory   18
The Car   19
Stupid   21
Union Street: San Francisco, Summer 1975   23
Bonnard's Nudes   25
Jean's TV   26
Mesopotamia   28
The Jungle   30
Hope   32
The House Behind This One   34
Limits   35
The Sensitive Girl   38

Two

The Minuet   43
Egress   44
Spell   46
From the East, Light   48

A Tall Order   50
The Author of Her Misfortune   51
Powder-Monkey   52
Earwigs   54
NyQuil   56
The Possible   57
Shiftless   59
The Young Fire Eaters of Mexico City   60
Where the Groceries Went   61
What I Can Do   63
The Little Room   64
Sweet Light   65
The Garden   66
Son   68
Kafka's Watch   69

Three

The Lightning Speed of the Past   73
Vigil   74
In the Lobby of the Hotel del Mayo   75
Bahia, Brazil   77
The Phenomenon   79
Wind   80
Migration   82
Sleeping   85
The River   86
The Best Time of the Day   87
Scale   88
Company   91
Yesterday   92
The Schooldesk   93
Cutlery   96
The Pen   98
The Prize   100
An Account   101
The Meadow   103
Loafing   105

Sinew   106
Waiting   108

Four

The Debate   111
Its Course   112
September   114
The White Field   115
Shooting   117
The Window   119
Heels   120
The Phone Booth   122
Cadillacs and Poetry   124
Simple   126
The Scratch   127
Mother   128
The Child   129
The Fields   130
After Reading *Two Towns in Provence*   132
Evening   133
The Rest   134
Slippers   135
Asia   137
The Gift   139

ONE

This Morning

This morning was something. A little snow
lay on the ground. The sun floated in a clear
blue sky. The sea was blue, and blue-green,
as far as the eye could see.
Scarcely a ripple. Calm. I dressed and went
for a walk—determined not to return
until I took in what Nature had to offer.
I passed close to some old, bent-over trees.
Crossed a field strewn with rocks
where snow had drifted. Kept going
until I reached the bluff.
Where I gazed at the sea, and the sky, and
the gulls wheeling over the white beach
far below. All lovely. All bathed in a pure
cold light. But, as usual, my thoughts
began to wander. I had to will
myself to see what I was seeing
and nothing else. I had to tell myself *this* is what
mattered, not the other. (And I did see it,
for a minute or two!) For a minute or two
it crowded out the usual musings on
what was right, and what was wrong—duty,
tender memories, thoughts of death, how I should treat
with my former wife. All the things
I hoped would go away this morning.
The stuff I live with every day. What
I've trampled on in order to stay alive.

But for a minute or two I did forget
myself and everything else. I know I did.
For when I turned back I didn't know
where I was. Until some birds rose up
from the gnarled trees. And flew
in the direction I needed to be going.

What You Need for Painting

from a letter by Renoir

THE PALETTE:

Flake white

Chrome yellow

Naples yellow

Yellow ocher

Raw umber

Venetian red

French vermilion

Madder lake

Rose madder

Cobalt blue

Ultramarine blue

Emerald green

Ivory black

Raw sienna

Viridian green

White lead

DON'T FORGET:

Palette knife

Scraping knife

Essence of turpentine

BRUSHES?

Pointed marten-hair brushes

Flat hog-hair brushes

Indifference to everything except your canvas.

The ability to work like a locomotive.

An iron will.

As he writes, without looking at the sea,
he feels the tip of his pen begin to tremble.
The tide is going out across the shingle.
But it isn't that. No,
it's because at that moment she chooses
to walk into the room without any clothes on.
Drowsy, not even sure where she is
for a moment. She waves the hair from her forehead.
Sits on the toilet with her eyes closed,
head down. Legs sprawled. He sees her
through the doorway. Maybe
she's remembering what happened that morning.
For after a time, she opens one eye and looks at him.
And sweetly smiles.

Circulation

And all at length are gathered in.
—LOUISE BOGAN

By the time I came around to feeling pain
and woke up, moonlight
flooded the room. My arm lay paralyzed,
propped like an old anchor under
your back. You were in a dream,
you said later, where you'd arrived
early for the dance. But after
a moment's anxiety you were okay
because it was really a sidewalk
sale, and the shoes you were wearing,
or not wearing, were fine for that.

"Help me," I said. And tried to hoist
my arm. But it just lay there, aching,
unable to rise on its own. Even after
you said "What is it? What's wrong?"
it stayed put—deaf, unmoved
by any expression of fear or amazement.
We shouted at it, and grew afraid
when it didn't answer. "It's gone to sleep,"
I said, and hearing those words
knew how absurd this was. But
I couldn't laugh. Somehow,
between the two of us, we managed
to raise it. *This can't be my arm*
is what I kept thinking as
we thumped it, squeezed it, and

prodded it back to life. Shook it
until that stinging went away.

We said a few words to each other.
I don't remember what. Whatever
reassuring things people
who love each other say to each other
given the hour and such odd
circumstance. I do remember
you remarked how it was light
enough in the room that you could see
circles under my eyes.
You said I needed more regular sleep,
and I agreed. Each of us went
to the bathroom, and climbed back in bed
on our respective sides.
Pulled the covers up. "Good night,"
you said, for the second time that night.
And fell asleep. Maybe
into that same dream, or else another.

I lay until daybreak, holding
both arms fast across my chest.
Working my fingers now and then.
While my thoughts kept circling
around and around, but always going back
where they'd started from.
That one inescapable fact: even while
we undertake this trip,
there's another, far more bizarre,
we still have to make.

The Cobweb

A few minutes ago, I stepped onto the deck
of the house. From there I could see and hear the water,
and everything that's happened to me all these years.
It was hot and still. The tide was out.
No birds sang. As I leaned against the railing
a cobweb touched my forehead.
It caught in my hair. No one can blame me that I turned
and went inside. There was no wind. The sea
was dead calm. I hung the cobweb from the lampshade.
Where I watch it shudder now and then when my breath
touches it. A fine thread. Intricate.
Before long, before anyone realizes,
I'll be gone from here.

Balsa Wood

My dad is at the stove in front of a pan with brains
and eggs. But who has any appetite
this morning? I feel flimsy as
balsa wood. Something has just been said.
My mom said it. What was it? Something,
I'll bet, that bears on money. I'll do my part
if I don't eat. Dad turns his back on the stove.
"I'm in a hole. Don't dig me deeper."
Light leaks in from the window. Someone's crying.
The last thing I recall is the smell
of burned brains and eggs. The whole morning
is shoveled into the garbage and mixed
with other things. Sometime later
he and I drive to the dump, ten miles out.
We don't talk. We throw our bags and cartons
onto a dark mound. Rats screech.
They whistle as they crawl out of rotten sacks
dragging their bellies. We get back in the car
to watch the smoke and fire. The motor's running.
I smell the airplane glue on my fingers.
He looks at me as I bring my fingers to my nose.
Then looks away again, toward town.
He wants to say something but can't.
He's a million miles away. We're both far away
from there, and still someone's crying. Even then
I was beginning to understand how it's possible
to be in one place. And someplace else, too.

The Projectile

for Haruki Murakami

We sipped tea. Politely musing
on possible reasons for the success
of my books in your country. Slipped
into talk of pain and humiliation
you find occurring, and reoccurring,
in my stories. And that element
of sheer chance. How all this translates
in terms of sales.
I looked into a corner of the room.
And for a minute I was 16 again,
careening around in the snow
in a '50 Dodge sedan with five or six
bozos. Giving the finger
to some other bozos, who yelled and pelted
our car with snowballs, gravel, old
tree branches. We spun away, shouting.
And we were going to leave it at that.
But my window was down three inches.
Only three inches. I hollered out
one last obscenity. And saw this guy
wind up to throw. From this vantage,
now, I imagine I see it coming. See it
speeding through the air while I watch,
like those soldiers in the first part
of the last century watched canisters
of shot fly in their direction
while they stood, unable to move

for the dread fascination of it.
But I *didn't* see it. I'd already turned
my head to laugh with my pals.
When something slammed into the side
of my head so hard it broke my eardrum and fell
in my lap, intact. A ball of packed ice
and snow. The pain was stupendous.
And the humiliation.
It was awful when I began to weep
in front of those tough guys while they
cried, *Dumb luck. Freak accident.*
A chance in a million!
The guy who threw it, he had to be amazed
and proud of himself while he took
the shouts and backslaps of the others.
He must have wiped his hands on his pants.
And messed around a little more
before going home to supper. He grew up
to have his share of setbacks and got lost
in his life, same as I got lost in mine.
He never gave that afternoon
another thought. And why should he?
So much else to think about always.
Why remember that stupid car sliding
down the road, then turning the corner
and disappearing?
We politely raise our teacups in the room.
A room that for a minute something else entered.

The Mail

On my desk, a picture postcard from my son
in southern France. The Midi,
he calls it. Blue skies. Beautiful houses
loaded with begonias. Nevertheless
he's going under, needs money fast.

Next to his card, a letter
from my daughter telling me her old man,
the speed-freak, is tearing down
a motorcycle in the living room.
They're existing on oatmeal,
she and her children. For God's sake,
she could use some help.

And there's the letter from my mother
who is sick and losing her mind.
She tells me she won't be here
much longer. Won't I help her make
this one last move? Can't I pay
for her to have a home of her own?

I go outside. Thinking to walk
to the graveyard for some comfort.
But the sky is in turmoil.
The clouds, huge and swollen with darkness,
about to spew open.
It's then the postman turns into

the drive. His face
is a reptile's, glistening and working.
His hand goes back—as if to strike!
It's the mail.

The Autopsy Room

Then I was young and had the strength of ten.
For anything, I thought. Though part of my job
at night was to clean the autopsy room
once the coroner's work was done. But now
and then they knocked off early, or too late.
For, so help me, they left things out
on their specially built table. A little baby,
still as a stone and snow cold. Another time,
a huge black man with white hair whose chest
had been laid open. All his vital organs
lay in a pan beside his head. The hose
was running, the overhead lights blazed.
And one time there was a leg, a woman's leg,
on the table. A pale and shapely leg.
I knew it for what it was. I'd seen them before.
Still, it took my breath away.

When I went home at night my wife would say,
"Sugar, it's going to be all right. We'll trade
this life in for another." But it wasn't
that easy. She'd take my hand between her hands
and hold it tight, while I leaned back on the sofa
and closed my eyes. Thinking of . . . something.
I don't know what. But I'd let her bring
my hand to her breast. At which point
I'd open my eyes and stare at the ceiling, or else
the floor. Then my fingers strayed to her leg.

Which was warm and shapely, ready to tremble and raise slightly, at the slightest touch.
But my mind was unclear and shaky. Nothing was happening. Everything was happening. Life was a stone, grinding and sharpening.

Where They'd Lived

Everywhere he went that day he walked
in his own past. Kicked through piles
of memories. Looked through windows
that no longer belonged to him.
Work and poverty and short change.
In those days they'd lived by their wills,
determined to be invincible.
Nothing could stop them. Not
for the longest while.

                  In the motel room
that night, in the early morning hours,
he opened a curtain. Saw clouds
banked against the moon. He leaned
closer to the glass. Cold air passed
through and put its hand over his heart.
I loved you, he thought.
Loved you well.
Before loving you no longer.

Memory

She lays her hand on his shoulder
at the checkout stand. But he won't
go with her, and shakes his head.

She insists! He pays. She walks out
with him to his big car, takes one look,
laughs at it. Touches his cheek.

Leaves him with his groceries
in the parking lot. Feeling foolish.
Feeling diminished. Still paying.

The Car

The car with a cracked windshield.
The car that threw a rod.
The car without brakes.
The car with a faulty U-joint.
The car with a hole in its radiator.
The car I picked peaches for.
The car with a cracked block.
The car with no reverse gear.
The car I traded for a bicycle.
The car with steering problems.
The car with generator trouble.
The car with no back seat.
The car with the torn front seat.
The car that burned oil.
The car with rotten hoses.
The car that left the restaurant without paying.
The car with bald tires.
The car with no heater or defroster.
The car with its front end out of alignment.
The car the child threw up in.
The car *I* threw up in.
The car with the broken water pump.
The car whose timing gear was shot.
The car with a blown head-gasket.
The car I left on the side of the road.
The car that leaked carbon monoxide.
The car with a sticky carburetor.

The car that hit the dog and kept going.
The car with a hole in its muffler.
The car with no muffler.
The car my daughter wrecked.
The car with the twice-rebuilt engine.
The car with corroded battery cables.
The car bought with a bad check.
Car of my sleepless nights.
The car with a stuck thermostat.
The car whose engine caught fire.
The car with no headlights.
The car with a broken fan belt.
The car with wipers that wouldn't work.
The car I gave away.
The car with transmission trouble.
The car I washed my hands of.
The car I struck with a hammer.
The car with payments that couldn't be met.
The repossessed car.
The car whose clutch-pin broke.
The car waiting on the back lot.
Car of my dreams.
My car.

Stupid

It's what the kids nowadays call weed. And it drifts
like clouds from his lips. He hopes no one
comes along tonight, or calls to ask for help.
Help is what he's most short on tonight.
A storm thrashes outside. Heavy seas
with gale winds from the west. The table he sits at
is, say, two cubits long and one wide.
The darkness in the room teems with insight.
Could be he'll write an adventure novel. Or else
a children's story. A play for two female characters,
one of whom is blind. Cutthroat should be coming
into the river. One thing he'll do is learn
to tie his own flies. Maybe he should give
more money to each of his surviving
family members. The ones who already expect a little
something in the mail first of each month.
Every time they write they tell him
they're coming up short. He counts heads on his fingers
and finds they're all surviving. So what
if he'd rather be remembered in the dreams of strangers?
He raises his eyes to the skylights where rain
hammers on. After a while—
who knows how long?—his eyes ask
that they be closed. And he closes them.
But the rain keeps hammering. Is this a cloudburst?
Should he do something? Secure the house
in some way? Uncle Bo stayed married to Aunt Ruby

for 47 years. Then hanged himself.
He opens his eyes again. Nothing adds up.
It all adds up. How long will this storm go on?

Union Street: San Francisco, Summer 1975

In those days we were going places. But that Sunday
afternoon we were becalmed. Sitting around a table,
drinking and swapping stories. A party that'd been
going on, and off, since Friday a year ago.
Then Guy's wife was dropped off in front of the apartment
by her boyfriend, and came upstairs.
It's Guy's birthday, after all, give or take a day.
They haven't seen each other for a week,
more or less. She's all dressed up. He embraces her,
sort of, makes her a drink. Finds a place
for her at the table. Everyone wants to know
how she is, etc. But she ignores them all.
All those alcoholics. Clearly, she's pissed off
and as usual in the wrong company.
Where the hell has Guy been keeping himself?
she wants to know. She sips her drink and looks at him
as if he's brain-damaged. She spots a pimple
on his chin; it's an ingrown hair but it's filled
with pus, frightful, looks like hell. In front
of everyone she says, "Who have *you* been eating out
lately?" Staring hard at his pimple.
Being drunk myself, I don't recall how he answered.
Maybe he said, "I don't remember who it was;
I didn't get her name." Something smart.
Anyway, his wife has this kind of blistery rash,
maybe it's cold sores, at the edge of her mouth,
so she shouldn't be talking. Pretty soon,

it's like always: they're holding hands and laughing
like the rest of us, at little or nothing.

Later, in the living room,
thinking everyone had gone out for hamburgers,
she blew him in front of the TV. Then said,
"Happy birthday, you son of a bitch!" And slapped his
glasses off. The glasses he'd been wearing
while she made love to him. I walked into the room
and said, "Friends, don't do this to each other."
She didn't flinch a muscle or wonder aloud
which rock I'd come out from under. All she said was
"Who asked you, hobo-urine?" Guy put his glasses on.
Pulled his trousers up. We all went out
to the kitchen and had a drink. Then another. Like that,
the world had gone from afternoon to night.

Bonnard's Nudes

His wife. Forty years he painted her.
Again and again. The nude in the last painting
the same young nude as the first. His wife.

As he remembered her young. As she was young.
His wife in her bath. At her dressing table
in front of the mirror. Undressed.

His wife with her hands under her breasts
looking out on the garden.
The sun bestowing warmth and color.

Every living thing in bloom there.
She young and tremulous and most desirable.
When she died, he painted a while longer.

A few landscapes. Then died.
And was put down next to her.
His young wife.

My life's on an even keel
these days. Though who's to say
it'll never waver again?
This morning I recalled
a girl friend I had just after
my marriage broke up.
A sweet girl named Jean.
In the beginning, she had no idea
how bad things were. It took
a while. But she loved me
a bunch anyway, she said.

And I know that's true.
She let me stay at her place
where I conducted
the shabby business of my life
over her phone. She bought
my booze, but told me
I wasn't a drunk
like those others said.
Signed checks for me
and left them on her pillow
when she went off to work.
Gave me a Pendleton jacket
that Christmas, one I still wear.

For my part, I taught her to drink.

And how to fall asleep
with her clothes on.
How to wake up
weeping in the middle of the night.
When I left, she paid two months'
rent for me. And gave me
her black and white TV.

We talked on the phone once,
months later. She was drunk.
And, sure, I was drunk too.
The last thing she said to me was,
Will I ever see my TV again?
I looked around the room
as if the TV might suddenly
appear in its place
on the kitchen chair. Or else
come out of a cupboard
and declare itself. But that TV
had gone down the road
weeks before. The TV Jean gave me.

I didn't tell her that.
I lied, of course. Soon, I said,
very soon now.
And put down the phone
after, or before, she hung up.
But those sleep-sounding words
of mine making me feel
I'd come to the end of a story.
And now, this one last falsehood
behind me,
     I could rest.

Mesopotamia

Waking before sunrise, in a house not my own,
I hear a radio playing in the kitchen.
Mist drifts outside the window while
a woman's voice gives the news, and then the weather.
I hear that, and the sound of meat
as it connects with hot grease in the pan.
I listen some more, half asleep. It's like,
but not like, when I was a child and lay in bed,
in the dark, listening to a woman crying,
and a man's voice raised in anger, or despair,
the radio playing all the while. Instead,
what I hear this morning is the man of the house
saying "How many summers do I have left?
Answer me that." There's no answer from the woman
that I can hear. But what *could* she answer,
given such a question? In a minute,
I hear his voice speaking of someone who I think
must be long gone: "That man could say,
   'O, Mesopotamia!'
and move his audience to tears."
I get out of bed at once and draw on my pants.
Enough light in the room that I can see
where I am, finally. I'm a grown man, after all,
and these people are my friends. Things
are not going well for them just now. Or else
they're going better than ever
because they're up early and talking

about such things of consequence
as death and Mesopotamia. In any case,
I feel myself being drawn to the kitchen.
So much that is mysterious and important
is happening out there this morning.

The Jungle

"I only have two hands,"
the beautiful flight attendant
says. She continues
up the aisle with her tray and
out of his life forever,
he thinks. Off to his left,
far below, some lights
from a village high
on a hill in the jungle.

So many impossible things
have happened,
he isn't surprised when she
returns to sit in the
empty seat across from his.
"Are you getting off
in Rio, or going on to Buenos Aires?"

Once more she exposes
her beautiful hands.
The heavy silver rings that hold
her fingers, the gold bracelet
encircling her wrist.

They are somewhere in the air
over the steaming Mato Grosso.
It is very late.

He goes on considering her hands.
Looking at her clasped fingers.
It's months afterwards, and
hard to talk about.

Hope

"My wife," said Pinnegar, *"expects to see me go to the dogs
when she leaves me. It is her last hope."*
—D. H. LAWRENCE,
"JIMMY AND THE DESPERATE WOMAN"

She gave me the car and two
hundred dollars. Said, So long, baby.
Take it easy, hear? So much
for twenty years of marriage.
She knows, or thinks she knows,
I'll go through the dough
in a day or two, and eventually
wreck the car—which was
in my name and needed work anyway.
When I drove off, she and her boy-
friend were changing the lock
on the front door. They waved.
I waved back to let them know
I didn't think any the less
of them. Then sped toward
the state line. I *was* hell-bent.
She was right to think so.

I went to the dogs, and we
became good friends.
But I kept going. Went
a long way without stopping.
Left the dogs, my friends, behind.
Nevertheless, when I did show
my face at that house again,
months, or years, later, driving
a different car, she wept

when she saw me at the door.
Sober. Dressed in a clean shirt,
pants, and boots. Her last hope
blasted.
She didn't have a thing
to hope for anymore.

The House Behind This One

The afternoon was already dark and unnatural.
When this old woman appeared in the field,
in the rain, carrying a bridle.
She came up the road to the house.
The house behind this one. Somehow
she knew Antonio Ríos had entered
the hour of his final combat.
Somehow, don't ask me how, she knew.

The doctor and some other people were with him.
But nothing more could be done. And so
the old woman carried the bridle into the room,
and hung it across the foot of his bed.
The bed where he writhed and lay dying.
She went away without a word.
This woman who'd once been young and beautiful.
When Antonio was young and beautiful.

All that day we banged at geese
from a blind at the top
of the bluff. Busted one flock
after the other, until our gun barrels
grew hot to the touch. Geese
filled the cold, grey air. But we still
didn't kill our limits.
The wind driving our shot
every whichway. Late afternoon,
and we had four. Two shy
of our limits. Thirst drove us
off the bluff and down a dirt road
alongside the river.

To an evil-looking farm
surrounded by dead fields of
barley. Where, almost evening,
a man with patches of skin
gone from his hands let us dip water
from a bucket on his porch.
Then asked if we wanted to see
something—a Canada goose he kept
alive in a barrel beside
the barn. The barrel covered over
with screen wire, rigged inside
like a little cell. He'd broken
the bird's wing with a long shot,

he said, then chased it down
and stuffed it in the barrel.
He'd had a brainstorm!
He'd use that goose as a live decoy.

In time it turned out to be
the damnedest thing he'd ever seen.
It would bring other geese
right down on your head.
So close you could almost touch them
before you killed them.
This man, he never wanted for geese.
And for this his goose was given
all the corn and barley
it could eat, and a barrel
to live in, and shit in.

I took a good long look and,
unmoving, the goose looked back.
Only its eyes telling me
it was alive. Then we left,
my friend and I. Still
willing to kill anything
that moved, anything that rose
over our sights. I don't
recall if we got anything else
that day. I doubt it.
It was almost dark anyhow.
No matter, now. But for years
and years afterwards, living
on a staple of bitterness, I
didn't forget that goose.
I set it apart from all the others,

living and dead. Came to understand
one can get used to anything,
and become a stranger to nothing.
Saw that betrayal is just another word
for loss, for hunger.

The Sensitive Girl

This is the fourth day I've been here.
But, no joke, there's a spider
on this pane of glass
that's been around even longer. It doesn't
move, but I know it's alive.

Fine with me that lights are coming on
in the valleys. It's pretty here,
and quiet. Cattle are being driven home.
If I listen, I can hear cowbells
and then the *slap-slap* of the driver's
stick. There's haze
over these lumpy Swiss hills. Below the house,
a race of water through the alders.
Jets of water tossed up,
sweet and hopeful.

There was a time
I would've died for love.
No more. That center wouldn't hold.
It collapsed. It gives off
no light. Its orbit
an orbit of weariness. But I worry
that time and wish I knew why.
Who wants to remember
when poverty and disgrace pushed
through the door, followed by a cop

to invest the scene
with horrible authority?
The latch was fastened, but
that never stopped anybody back then.
Hey, no one breathed in those days.
Ask her, if you don't believe me!
Assuming you could find her and
make her talk. That girl who dreamed
and sang. Who sometimes hummed
when she made love. The sensitive girl.
The one who cracked.

I'm a grown man now, and then some.
So how much longer do I have?
How much longer for that spider?
Where will he go, two days into fall,
the leaves dropping?

The cattle have entered their pen.
The man with the stick raises his arm.
Then closes and fastens the gate.

I find myself, at last, in perfect silence.
Knowing the little that is left.
Knowing I have to love it.
Wanting to love it. For both our sake.

TWO

The Minuet

Bright mornings.
Days when I want so much I want nothing.
Just this life, and no more. Still,
I hope no one comes along.
But if someone does, I hope it's her.
The one with the little diamond stars
at the toes of her shoes.
The girl I saw dance the minuet.
That antique dance.
The minuet. She danced that
the way it should be danced.
And the way she wanted.

Egress

I opened the old spiral notebook to see what I'd been
thinking in those days. There was one entry,
in a hand I didn't recognize as mine, but was mine.
All that paper I'd let go to waste back then!

Removing the door for Dr. Kurbitz.

What on earth could that possibly mean to me,
or anyone, today? Then I went back
to that time. To just after being married. How I earned
our daily bread delivering for Al Kurbitz,
the pharmacist. Whose brother Ken—Dr. Kurbitz
to me, the ear-nose-and-throat man—fell dead
one night after dinner, after
talking over some business deal. He died in the bathroom,
his body wedged between the door and toilet stool.
Blocking the way. First the *whump*
of a body hitting the floor, and then Mr. Kurbitz
and his snazzy sister-in-law shouting "Ken! Ken!"
and pushing on the bathroom door.

Mr. Kurbitz had to take the door off its hinges
with a screwdriver. It saved the ambulance drivers
a minute, maybe. He said his brother never knew
what hit him. Dead before he hit the floor.

Since then, I've seen doors removed from their hinges

many times, with and without the aid of screwdrivers.
But I'd forgotten about Dr. Kurbitz, and so much else
from that time. Never, until today, did I connect
this act with dying.

                              In those days, death,
if it happened, happened to others. Old people
belonging to my parents. Or else people of consequence.
People in a different income bracket, whose death
and removal had nothing to do with me, or mine.

We were living in Dr. Coglon's basement
apartment, and I was in love for the first time
ever. My wife was pregnant. We were thrilled
beyond measure or accounting for, given our mean
surroundings. And that, I'm saying, may be why
I never wrote more about Dr. Kurbitz,
his brother Al, or doors that had to be taken off
their hinges for the sake of dead people.

What the hell! Who needed death and notebooks? We
were young and happy. Death was coming, sure.
But for the old and worn-out. Or else people in books.
And, once in a while, the well-heeled professionals
I trembled before and said "Yes, Sir" to.

Spell

Between five and seven this evening,
I lay in the channel of sleep. Attached
to this world by nothing more than hope,
I turned in a current of dark dreams.
It was during this time the weather
underwent a metamorphosis.
Became deranged. What before had been
vile and shabby, but comprehensible,
became swollen and
unrecognizable. Something utterly vicious.

In my despairing mood, I didn't
need it. It was the last thing on earth
I wanted. So with all the power I could muster,
I sent it packing. Sent it down the coast
to a big river I know about. A river
able to deal with foul weather
like this. So what if the river has to flee
to higher ground? Give it a few days.
It'll find its way.

Then all will be as before. I swear
this won't be more than a bad memory, if that.
Why, this time next week I won't remember
what I was feeling when I wrote this.
I'll have forgotten I slept badly
and dreamed for a time this evening . . .

to wake at seven o'clock, look out
at the storm and, after that first shock—
take heart. Think long and hard
about what I want, what I could let go
or send away. And then do it!
Like that. With words, and signs.

From the East, Light

The house rocked and shouted all night.
Toward morning, grew quiet. The children,
looking for something to eat, make
their way through the crazy living room
in order to get to the crazy kitchen.
There's Father, asleep on the couch.
Sure they stop to look. Who wouldn't?
They listen to his violent snores
and understand that the old way of life
has begun once more. So what else is new?
But the real shocker, what makes them stare,
is that their Christmas tree has been turned over.
It lies on its side in front of the fireplace.
The tree they helped decorate.
It's wrecked now, icicles and candy canes
litter the rug. How'd a thing like this happen, anyway?
And they see Father has opened
his present from Mother. It's a length of rope
half-in, half-out of its pretty box.
Let them both go hang
themselves, is what they'd like to say.
To hell with it, and
them, is what they're thinking. Meanwhile,
there's cereal in the cupboard, milk
in the fridge. They take their bowls
in where the TV is, find their show,
try to forget about the mess everywhere.

Up goes the volume. Louder, and then louder. Father turns over and groans. The children laugh. They turn it up some more so he'll for sure know he's alive. He raises his head. Morning begins.

A Tall Order

This old woman who kept house for them,
she'd seen and heard the most amazing things.
Sights like plates and bottles flying.
An ashtray traveling like a missile
that hit the dog in the head.
Once she let herself in and found a huge
salad in the middle of the dining-room table.
It was sprinkled with moldy croutons.
The table was set for six, but nobody
had eaten. Dust filmed the cups and silver.
Upstairs a man pleaded
not to have his hair pulled by the roots again.
Please, please, please he cried.

Her job was to set the house in order.
At least make it like she'd left it last time.
That was all. Nobody asked her opinion,
and she didn't give it. She put on her apron.
Turned the hot water on full, drowning out
that other sound. Her arms went into the suds
to her elbows. She leaned on the counter.
And stared into the backyard where they kept
the rusty swing and jungle-gym set.
If she kept watching, she was sure to see
the elephant step out of the trees and trumpet
as it did every Monday at this house, at this hour.

The Author of Her Misfortune

For the world is the world.
And it writes no histories
that end in love.
—STEPHEN SPENDER

I'm not the man she claims. But
this much is true: the past is
distant, a receding coastline,
and we're all in the same boat,
a scrim of rain over the sea-lanes.
Still, I wish she wouldn't keep on
saying those things about me!
Over the long course
everything but hope lets you go, then
even that loosens its grip.
There isn't enough of anything
as long as we live. But at intervals
a sweetness appears and, given a chance,
prevails. It's true I'm happy now.
And it'd be nice if she
could hold her tongue. Stop
hating me for being happy.
Blaming me for her life. I'm afraid
I'm mixed up in her mind
with someone else. A young man
of no character, living on dreams,
who swore he'd love her forever.
One who gave her a ring, and a bracelet.
Who said, *Come with me. You can trust me.*
Things to that effect. I'm not that man.
She has me confused, as I said,
with someone else.

51

Powder-Monkey

When my friend John Dugan, the carpenter,
left this world for the next, he seemed
in a terrible hurry. He wasn't, of course.
Almost no one is. But he barely took time
to say goodbye. "I'll just put these tools away,"
he said. Then, "So long." And hurried
down the hill to his pickup. He waved, and
I waved. But between here and Dungeness,
where he used to live, he drifted
over the center line, onto Death's side.
And was destroyed by a logging truck.

                       He is working
under the sun with his shirt off, a blue
bandanna around his forehead to keep sweat from his eyes.
Driving nails. Drilling and planing lumber.
Joining wood together with other wood.
In every way taking the measure of this house.
Stopping to tell a story now and then,
about when he was a young squirt, working
as a powder-monkey. The close calls he'd had
laying fuses. His white teeth flashing when he laughs.
The blond handlebar mustache he loved to
pull on while musing. "So long," he said.

I want to imagine him riding unharmed
toward Death. Even though the fuse is burning.

Nothing to do there in the cab
of his pickup but listen to Ricky Skaggs,
pull on his mustache, and plan Saturday night.
This man with all Death before him.
Riding unharmed, and untouched,
toward Death.

Earwigs

for Mona Simpson

Your delicious-looking rum cake, covered with
almonds, was hand-carried to my door
this morning. The driver parked at the foot
of the hill, and climbed the steep path.
Nothing else moved in that frozen landscape.
It was cold inside and out. I signed
for it, thanked him, went back in.
Where I stripped off the heavy tape, tore
the staples from the bag, and inside
found the canister you'd filled with cake.
I scratched adhesive from the lid.
Prized it open. Folded back the aluminum foil.
To catch the first whiff of that sweetness!

It was then the earwig appeared
from the moist depths. An earwig
stuffed on your cake. Drunk
from it. He went over the side of the can.
Scurried wildly across the table to take
refuge in the fruit bowl. I didn't kill it.
Not then. Filled as I was with conflicting
feelings. Disgust, of course. But
amazement. Even admiration. This creature
that'd just made a 3,000-mile, overnight trip
by air, surrounded by cake, shaved almonds,
and the overpowering odor of rum. Carried
then in a truck over a mountain road and

packed uphill in freezing weather to a house
overlooking the Pacific Ocean. An earwig.
I'll let him live, I thought. What's one more,
or less, in the world? This one's special,
maybe. Blessings on its strange head.

I lifted the cake from its foil wrapping
and three more earwigs went over the side
of the can! For a minute I was so taken
aback I didn't know if I should kill them,
or what. Then rage seized me, and
I plastered them. Crushed the life from them
before any could get away. It was a massacre.
While I was at it, I found and destroyed
the other one utterly.
I was just beginning when it was all over.
I'm saying I could have gone on and on,
rending them. If it's true
that man is wolf to man, what can mere earwigs
expect when bloodlust is up?

I sat down, trying to quieten my heart.
Breath rushing from my nose. I looked
around the table, slowly. Ready
for anything. Mona, I'm sorry to say this,
but I couldn't eat any of your cake.
I've put it away for later, maybe.
Anyway, thanks. You're sweet to remember
me out here alone this winter.
Living alone.
Like an animal, I think.

NyQuil

Call it iron discipline. But for months
I never took my first drink
before eleven P.M. Not so bad,
considering. This was in the beginning
phase of things. I knew a man
whose drink of choice was Listerine.
He was coming down off Scotch.
He bought Listerine by the case,
and drank it by the case. The back seat
of his car was piled high with dead soldiers.
Those empty bottles of Listerine
gleaming in his scalding back seat!
The sight of it sent me home soul-searching.
I did that once or twice. Everybody does.
Go way down inside and look around.
I spent hours there, but
didn't meet anyone, or see anything
of interest. I came back to the here and now,
and put on my slippers. Fixed
myself a nice glass of NyQuil.
Dragged a chair over to the window.
Where I watched a pale moon struggle to rise
over Cupertino, California.
I waited through hours of darkness with NyQuil.
And then, sweet Jesus! the first sliver
of light.

I spent years, on and off, in academe.
Taught at places I couldn't get near
as a student. But never wrote a line
about that time. Never. Nothing stayed
with me in those days. I was a stranger,
and an impostor, even to myself. Except
at that one school. That distinguished
institution in the midwest. Where
my only friend, and my colleague,
the Chaucerian, was arrested for beating his wife.
And threatening her life over the phone,
a misdemeanor. He wanted to put her eyes out.
Set her on fire for cheating.
The guy she was seeing, he was going to hammer him
into the ground like a fence post.

He lost his mind for a time, while she moved away
to a new life. Thereafter, he taught
his classes weeping drunk. More than once
wore his lunch on his shirt front.
I was no help. I was fading fast myself.
But seeing the way he was living, so to speak,
I understood I hadn't strayed so far from home
after all. My scholar-friend. My old pal.
At long last I'm out of all that.
And you. I pray your hands are steady,
and that you're happy tonight. I hope some woman

has just put her hand under your clean collar
a minute ago, and told you she loves you.
Believe her, if you can, for it's possible she means it.
Is someone who will be true, and kind to you.
All your remaining days.

Shiftless

The people who were better than us were *comfortable*.
They lived in painted houses with flush toilets.
Drove cars whose year and make were recognizable.
The ones worse off were *sorry* and didn't work.
Their strange cars sat on blocks in dusty yards.
The years go by and everything and everyone
gets replaced. But this much is still true—
I never liked work. My goal was always
to be shiftless. I saw the merit in that.
I liked the idea of sitting in a chair
in front of your house for hours, doing nothing
but wearing a hat and drinking cola.
What's wrong with that?
Drawing on a cigarette from time to time.
Spitting. Making things out of wood with a knife.
Where's the harm there? Now and then calling
the dogs to hunt rabbits. Try it sometime.
Once in a while hailing a fat, blond kid like me
and saying, "Don't I know you?"
Not, "What are you going to be when you grow up?"

The Young Fire Eaters of Mexico City

They fill their mouths with alcohol
and blow it over a lighted candle
at traffic signs. Anyplace, really,
where cars line up and the drivers
are angry and frustrated and looking
for distraction—there you'll find
the young fire eaters. Doing what they do
for a few pesos. If they're lucky.
But in a year their lips
are scorched and their throats raw.
They have no voice within a year.
They can't talk or cry out—
these silent children who hunt
through the streets with a candle
and a beer can filled with alcohol.
They are called *milusos*. Which translates
into "a thousand uses."

Where the Groceries Went

When his mother called for the second time
that day, she said:
"I don't have any strength left. I want
to lay down all the time."

"Did you take your iron?" he wanted to know.
He sincerely wanted to know. Praying daily,
hopelessly, that iron might make a difference.
"Yes, but it just makes me hungry. And I don't
have anything to eat."

He pointed out to her they'd shopped
for hours that morning. Brought home
eighty dollars' worth of food to stack
in her cupboards and the fridge.
"There's nothing to eat in this goddamn house
but baloney and cheese," she said.
Her voice shook with anger. "Nothing!"
"And how's your cat? How's Kitty doing?"
His own voice shook. He needed
to get off this subject of food; it never
brought them anything but grief.

"Kitty," his mother said. "Here, Kitty.
Kitty, Kitty. She won't answer me, honey.
I don't know this for sure, but I think
she jumped into the washing machine

when I was about to do a load. And before I forget,
that machine's making
a banging noise. I think there's something
the matter with it. Kitty! She won't
answer me. Honey, I'm afraid.
I'm afraid of everything. Help me, please.
Then you can go back to whatever it was
you were doing. Whatever
it was that was so important
I had to take the trouble
to bring you into this world."

What I Can Do

All I want today is to keep an eye on these birds
outside my window. The phone is unplugged
so my loved ones can't reach out and put the arm
on me. I've told them the well has run dry.
They won't hear of it. They keep trying
to get through anyway. Just now I can't bear to know
about the car that blew another gasket.
Or the trailer I thought I'd paid for long ago,
now foreclosed on. Or the son in Italy
who threatens to end his life there
unless I keep paying the bills. My mother wants
to talk to me too. Wants to remind me again how it was
back then. All the milk I drank, cradled in her arms.
That ought to be worth something now. She needs
me to pay for this new move of hers. She'd like
to loop back to Sacramento for the twentieth time.
Everybody's luck has gone south. All I ask
is to be allowed to sit for a moment longer.
Nursing a bite the shelty dog Keeper gave me last night.
And watching these birds. Who don't ask for a thing
except sunny weather. In a minute
I'll have to plug in the phone and try to separate
what's right from wrong. Until then
a dozen tiny birds, no bigger than teacups,
perch in the branches outside the window.
Suddenly they stop singing and turn their heads.
It's clear they've felt something.
They dive into flight.

The Little Room

There was a great reckoning.
Words flew like stones through windows.
She yelled and yelled, like the Angel of Judgment.

Then the sun shot up, and a contrail
appeared in the morning sky.
In the sudden silence, the little room
became oddly lonely as he dried her tears.
Became like all the other little rooms on earth
light finds hard to penetrate.

Rooms where people yell and hurt each other.
And afterwards feel pain, and loneliness.
Uncertainty. The need to comfort.

Sweet Light

After the winter, grieving and dull,
I flourished here all spring. Sweet light

began to fill my chest. I pulled up
a chair. Sat for hours in front of the sea.

Listened to the buoy and learned
to tell the difference between a bell,

and the sound of a bell. I wanted
everything behind me. I even wanted

to become inhuman. And I did that.
I know I did. (She'll back me up on this.)

I remember the morning I closed the lid
on memory and turned the handle.

Locking it away forever.
Nobody knows what happened to me

out here, sea. Only you and I know.
At night, clouds form in front of the moon.

By morning they're gone. And that sweet light
I spoke of? That's gone too.

The Garden

In the garden, small laughter from years ago.
Lanterns burning in the willows.
The power of those four words, "I loved a woman."
Put that on the stone beside his name.
God keep you and be with you.

Those horses coming into the stretch at Ruidoso!
Mist rising from the meadow at dawn.
From the veranda, the blue outlines of the mountains.
What used to be within reach, out of reach.
And in some lesser things, just the opposite is true.

Order anything you want! Then look for the man
with the limp to go by. He'll pay.
From a break in the wall, I could look down
on the shanty lights in the Valley of Kidron.
Very little sleep under strange roofs. His life far away.

Playing checkers with my dad. Then he hunts up
the shaving soap, the brush and bowl, the straight
razor, and we drive to the county hospital. I watch him
lather my grandpa's face. Then shave him.
The dying body is a clumsy partner.

Drops of water in your hair.
The dark yellow of the fields, the black and blue rivers.
Going out for a walk means you intend to return, right?

Eventually.
The flame is guttering. Marvelous.

The meeting between Goethe and Beethoven
took place in Leipzig in 1812. They talked into the night
about Lord Byron and Napoleon.
She got off the road and from then on it was nothing
But hardpan all the way.

She took a stick and in the dust drew the house where
they'd live and raise their children.
There was a duck pond and a place for horses.
To write about it, one would have to write in a way
that would stop the heart and make one's hair stand on end.

Cervantes lost a hand in the Battle of Lepanto.
This was in 1571, the last great sea battle fought
in ships manned by galley slaves.
In the Unuk River, in Ketchikan, the backs of the salmon
under the street lights as they come through town.

Students and young people chanted a requiem
as Tolstoy's coffin was carried across the yard
of the stationmaster's house at Astapovo and placed
in the freight car. To the accompaniment of singing,
the train slowly moved off.

A hard sail and the same stars everywhere.
But the garden is right outside my window.
Don't worry your heart about me, my darling.
We weave the thread given to us.
And Spring is with me.

Son

Awakened this morning by a voice from my childhood
that says *Time to get up,* I get up.
All night long, in my sleep, trying
to find a place where my mother could live
and be happy. *If you want me to lose my mind,*
the voice says *okay. Otherwise,*
get me out of here! I'm the one to blame
for moving her to this town she hates. Renting
her the house she hates.
Putting those neighbors she hates so close.
Buying the furniture she hates.
Why didn't you give me money instead, and let me spend it?
I want to go back to California, the voice says.
I'll die if I stay here. Do you want me to die?
There's no answer to this, or to anything else
in the world this morning. The phone rings
and rings. I can't go near it for fear
of hearing my name once more. The same name
my father answered to for 53 years.
Before going to his reward.
He died just after saying "Take this
into the kitchen, son."
The word *son* issuing from his lips.
Wobbling in the air for all to hear.

Kafka's Watch

from a letter

I have a job with a tiny salary of 80 crowns, and
an infinite eight to nine hours of work.
I devour the time outside the office like a wild beast.
Someday I hope to sit in a chair in another
country, looking out the window at fields of sugarcane
or Mohammedan cemeteries.
I don't complain about the work so much as about
the sluggishness of swampy time. The office hours
cannot be divided up! I feel the pressure
of the full eight or nine hours even in the last
half hour of the day. It's like a train ride
lasting night and day. In the end you're totally
crushed. You no longer think about the straining
of the engine, or about the hills or
flat countryside, but ascribe all that's happening
to your watch alone. The watch which you continually hold
in the palm of your hand. Then shake. And bring slowly
to your ear in disbelief.

THREE

The Lightning Speed of the Past

*The corpse fosters anxiety in men who believe
in the Last Judgment, and those who don't.*
—ANDRÉ MALRAUX

He buried his wife, who'd died in
misery. In misery, he
took to his porch, where he watched
the sun set and the moon rise.
The days seemed to pass, only to return
again. Like a dream in which one thinks,
I've already dreamt that.

Nothing, having arrived, will stay.
With his knife he cut the skin
from an apple. The white pulp, body
of the apple, darkened
and turned brown, then black,
before his eyes. The worn-out face of death!
The lightning speed of the past.

Vigil

They waited all day for the sun to appear. Then,
late in the afternoon, like a good prince,
it showed itself for a few minutes.
Blazing high over the benchland that lies at the foot
of the peaks behind their borrowed house.
Then the clouds were drawn once more.

They were happy enough. But all evening
the curtains made melancholy gestures,
swishing in front of the open windows. After dinner
they stepped onto the balcony.
Where they heard the river plunging in the canyon and,
closer, the creak of trees, sigh of boughs.

The tall grasses promised to rustle forever.
She put her hand on his neck. He touched her cheek.
Then bats came from all sides to harry them back.
Inside, they closed the windows. Kept their distance.
Watched a procession of stars. And, once in a while,
creatures that flung themselves in front of the moon.

In the Lobby of the Hotel del Mayo

The girl in the lobby reading a leather-bound book.
The man in the lobby using a broom.
The boy in the lobby watering plants.
The desk clerk looking at his nails.
The woman in the lobby writing a letter.
The old man in the lobby sleeping in his chair.
The fan in the lobby revolving slowly overhead.
Another hot Sunday afternoon.

Suddenly, the girl lays her finger between the pages of
    her book.
The man leans on his broom and looks.
The boy stops in his tracks.
The desk clerk raises his eyes and stares.
The woman quits writing.
The old man stirs and wakes up.
What is it?

Someone is running up from the harbor.
Someone who has the sun behind him.
Someone who is barechested.
Waving his arms.

It's clear something terrible has happened.
The man is running straight for the hotel.
His lips are working themselves into a scream.

Everyone in the lobby will recall their terror.
Everyone will remember this moment for the rest of
their lives.

Bahia, Brazil

The wind is level now. But pails of rain
fell today, and the day before,
and the day before that, all the way back
to Creation. The buildings
in the old slave quarter are dissolving,
and nobody cares. Not the ghosts
of the old slaves, or the young.
The water feels good on their whipped backs.
They could cry with relief.

No sunsets in this place. Light one minute,
and then the stars come out.
We could look all night in vain
for the Big Dipper. Down here
the Southern Cross is our sign.
I'm sick of the sound of my own voice!
Uneasy, and dreaming
of rum that could split my skull open.

There's a body lying on the stairs.
Step over it. The lights in the tower
have gone out. A spider hops from the man's
hair. This life. I'm saying it's one
amazing thing after the other.

Lines of men in the street,
as opposed to lines of poetry.

Choose! Are you guilty or not guilty?
What else have you? he answered.
Well, say the house was burning.
Would you save the cat or the Rembrandt?
That's easy. I don't have a Rembrandt,
and I don't have a cat. But I have
a sorrel horse back home
that I want to ride once more
into the high country.

Soon enough we'll rot under the earth.
No truth to this, just a fact.
We who gave each other so much
happiness while alive—
we're going to rot. But we won't
rot in this place. Not here.
Arms shackled together.
Jesus, the very idea of such a thing!
This life. These shackles.
I shouldn't bring it up.

The Phenomenon

I woke up feeling wiped out. God knows
where I've been all night, but my feet hurt.
Outside my window, a phenomenon is taking place.
The sun and moon hang side-by-side over the water.
Two sides of the same coin. I climb from bed
slowly, much as an old man might maneuver
from his musty bed in midwinter, finding it difficult
for a moment even to make water! I tell myself
this has to be a temporary condition.
In a few years, no problem. But when I look out
the window again, there's a sudden swoop of feeling.
Once more I'm arrested with the beauty of this place.
I was lying if I ever said anything to the contrary.
I move closer to the glass and see it's happened
between this thought and that. The moon
is gone. Set, at last.

Wind

for Richard Ford

Water perfectly calm. Perfectly amazing.
Flocks of birds moving
restlessly. Mystery enough in that, God knows.

You ask if I have the time. I do.
Time to go in. Fish not biting
anyway. Nothing doing anywhere.

When, a mile away, we see wind
moving across the water. Sit quiet and
watch it come. Nothing to worry about.

Just wind. Not so strong. Though strong enough.
You say, "Look at that!"
And we hold on to the gunwales as it passes.

I feel it fan my face and ears. Feel it
ruffle my hair—sweeter, it seems,
than any woman's fingers.

Then turn my head and watch
it move on down the Strait,
driving waves before it.

Leaving waves to flop against
our hull. The birds going crazy now.

Boat rocking from side to side.

"Jesus," you say, "I never saw anything like it."
"Richard," I say—
"You'll never see that in Manhattan, my friend."

Migration

A late summer's day, and my friend on the court
with his friend. Between games, the other remarks
how my friend's step seems not to have any spring
to it. His serve isn't so hot, either.
"You feeling okay?" he asks. "You had a checkup
lately?" Summer, and the living is easy.
But my friend went to see a doctor friend of his.
Who took his arm and gave him three months, no longer.

When I saw him a day later, it
was in the afternoon. He was watching TV.
He looked the same, but—how should I say it?—
different. He was embarrassed about the TV
and turned the sound down a little. But he couldn't
sit still. He circled the room, again and again.
"It's a program on animal migration," he said, as if this
might explain everything.
I put my arms around him and gave him a hug.
Not the really big hug I was capable of. Being afraid
that one of us, or both, might go to pieces.
And there was the momentary, crazy and dishonorable
    thought—
this might be catching.

I asked for an ashtray, and he was happy
to range around the house until he found one.
We didn't talk. Not then. Together we finished watching

the show. Reindeer, polar bears, fish, waterfowl,
butterflies and more. Sometimes they went from one
continent, or ocean, to another. But it was hard
to pay attention to the story taking place on screen.
My friend stood, as I recall, the whole time.

Was he feeling okay? He felt fine. He just couldn't
seem to stay still, was all. Something came into his eyes
and went away again. "What in hell are they talking about?"
he wanted to know. But didn't wait for an answer.
Began to walk some more. I followed him awkwardly
from room to room while he remarked on the weather,
his job, his ex-wife, his kids. Soon, he guessed,
he'd have to tell them . . . something.
"Am I really going to die?"

What I remember most about that awful day
was his restlessness, and my cautious hugs—*hello, goodbye.*
He kept moving until
we reached the front door and stopped.
He peered out, and drew back as if astounded
it could be light outside. A bank of shadow
from his hedge blocked the drive. And shadow fell
from the garage onto his lawn. He walked me to the car.
Our shoulders bumped. We shook hands, and I hugged him
once more. Lightly. Then he turned and went back,
passing quickly inside, closing the door. His face
appeared behind the window, then was gone.

He'll be on the move from now on. Traveling night and day,
without cease, all of him, every last exploding piece
of him. Until he reaches a place only he knows about.

An Arctic place, cold and frozen. Where he thinks,
This is far enough. This is the place.
And lies down, for he is tired.

He slept on his hands.
On a rock.
On his feet.
On someone else's feet.
He slept on buses, trains, in airplanes.
Slept on duty.
Slept beside the road.
Slept on a sack of apples.
He slept in a pay toilet.
In a hayloft.
In the Super Dome.
Slept in a Jaguar, and in the back of a pickup.
Slept in theaters.
In jail.
On boats.
He slept in line shacks and, once, in a castle.
Slept in the rain.
In blistering sun he slept.
On horseback.
He slept in chairs, churches, in fancy hotels.
He slept under strange roofs all his life.
Now he sleeps under the earth.
Sleeps on and on.
Like an old king.

The River

I waded, deepening, into the dark water.
Evening, and the push
and swirl of the river as it closed
around my legs and held on.
Young grilse broke water.
Parr darted one way, smolt another.
Gravel turned under my boots as I edged out.
Watched by the furious eyes of king salmon.
Their immense heads turned slowly,
eyes burning with fury, as they hung
in the deep current.
They were there. I felt them there,
and my skin prickled. But
there was something else.
I braced with the wind on my neck.
Felt the hair rise
as something touched my boot.
Grew afraid at what I couldn't see.
Then of everything that filled my eyes—
that other shore heavy with branches,
the dark lip of the mountain range behind.
And this river that had suddenly
grown black and swift.
I drew breath and cast anyway.
Prayed nothing would strike.

The Best Time of the Day

Cool summer nights.
Windows open.
Lamps burning.
Fruit in the bowl.
And your head on my shoulder.
These the happiest moments in the day.

Next to the early morning hours,
of course. And the time
just before lunch.
And the afternoon, and
early evening hours.
But I do love

These summer nights.
Even more, I think,
than those other times.
The work finished for the day.
And no one who can reach us now.
Or ever.

Scale

for Richard Marius

It's afternoon when he takes off
his clothes and lies down.
Lights his cigarette. Ashtray
balanced over his heart.
The chest rising, then
sinking
as he draws, holds it,
and lets the smoke out in spurts.
The shades are drawn. His eyelids
closing. It's like after sex,
a little. But only a little.
Waves thrash below the house.
He finishes the cigarette.
All the while thinking
of Thomas More who,
according to Erasmus, "liked eggs"
and never lay with his second wife.

The head stares down at its trunk
until it thinks it has it
memorized and could recognize
it anywhere, even in death.
But now the desire to sleep
has left him, utterly.
He is still remembering More
and his hair shirt. After thirty years of wear
he handed it over, along with his cloak,

before embracing his executioner.

He gets up to raise the shades.
Light slices the room in two.
A boat slowly rounds the hook
with its sails lowered.
There's a milky haze
over the water. A silence there.
It's much too quiet.
Even the birds are still.
Somewhere, off in another room,
something has been decided.
A decision reached, papers signed
and pushed aside.

He keeps on staring at the boat.
The empty rigging, the deserted deck.
The boat rises. Moves closer.
He peers through the glasses.
The human figure, the music
it makes, that's what's missing
from the tiny deck.
A deck no broader than a leaf.
So how could it support a life?

Suddenly, the boat shudders.
Stops dead in the water.
He sweeps the glasses over the deck.
But after a while his arms grow
unbearably heavy. So he drops them,
just as he would anything unbearable.
He lays the glasses on the shelf.
Begins dressing. But the image

of the boat stays. Drifting.
Stays awhile longer. Then bobs away.
Forgotten about as he takes up
his coat. Opens the door. Goes out.

Company

This morning I woke up to rain
on the glass. And understood
that for a long time now
I've chosen the corrupt when
I had a choice. Or else,
simply, the merely easy.
Over the virtuous. Or the difficult.
This way of thinking happens
when I've been alone for days.
Like now. Hours spent
in my own dumb company.
Hours and hours
much like a little room.
With just a strip of carpet to walk on.

Yesterday

Yesterday I dressed in a dead man's
woolen underwear. Then drove to the end
of an icy road where I passed
some time with Indian fishermen.
I stepped into water over my boots.
Saw four pintails spring from the creek.
Never mind that my thoughts were elsewhere
and I missed the perfect shot.
Or that my socks froze. I lost track
of everything and didn't make it back
for lunch. You could say
it wasn't my day. But it was!
And to prove it I have this little bite
she gave me last night. A bruise
coloring my lip today, to remind me.

The Schooldesk

The fishing in Lough Arrow is piss-poor.
Too much rain, too much high water.
They say the mayfly hatch has come
and gone. All day I stay put
by the window of the borrowed cottage
in Ballindoon, waiting for a break
in the weather. A turf fire smokes
in the grate, though no romance
in this or anything else
here. Just outside the window an old iron
and wood schooldesk keeps me company.
Something is carved into the desk under
the inkwell. It doesn't matter
what; I'm not curious. It's enough
to imagine the instrument
that gouged those letters.

        My dad is dead,
and Mother slips in and out of her mind.
I can't begin to say how bad it is
for my grown-up son and daughter.
They took one long look at me
and tried to make all my mistakes.
More's the pity. Bad luck for them,
my sweet children. And haven't I mentioned
my first wife yet? What's wrong with me
that I haven't? Well, I can't anymore.

Shouldn't, anyway. She claims
I say too much as it is.
Says she's happy now, and grinds her teeth.
Says the Lord Jesus loves her,
and she'll get by. That love
of my life over and done with. But what
does that say about my life?
My loved ones are thousands of miles away.
But they're in this cottage too,
in Ballindoon. And in every
hotel room I wake up in these days.

The rain has let up.
And the sun has appeared and small
clouds of unexpected mayflies,
proving someone wrong. We move
to the door in a group, my family and I.
And go outside. Where I bend over the desk
and run my fingers across its rough surface.
Someone laughs, someone grinds her teeth.
And someone, someone is pleading with me.
Saying, "For Christ's sake, don't
turn your back on me."

An ass and cart pass down the lane.
The driver takes the pipe from his mouth
and raises his hand.
There's the smell of lilacs in the damp air.
Mayflies hover over the lilacs,
and over the heads of my loved ones.
Hundreds of mayflies.
I sit on the bench. Lean
over the desk. I can remember

myself with a pen. In the beginning,
looking at pictures of words.
Learning to write them, slowly,
one letter at a time. Pressing down.
A word. Then the next.
The feeling of mastering something.
The excitement of it.
Pressing hard. At first
the damage confined to the surface.
But then deeper.

These blossoms. Lilacs.
How they fill the air with sweetness!
Mayflies in the air as the cart
goes by—as the fish rise.

Cutlery

Trolling the coho fly twenty feet behind the boat,
under moonlight, when the huge salmon hit it!
And lunged clear of the water. Stood, it seemed,
on its tail. Then fell back and was gone.
Shaken, I steered on into the harbor as if
nothing had happened. But it had.
And it happened in just the way I've said.
I took the memory with me to New York,
and beyond. Took it wherever I went.
All the way down here onto the terrace
of the Jockey Club in Rosario, Argentina.
Where I look out onto the broad river
that throws back light from the open windows
of the dining room. I stand smoking a cigar,
listening to the murmuring of the officers
and their wives inside; the little clashing
sound of cutlery against plates. I'm alive
and well, neither happy nor unhappy,
here in the Southern Hemisphere. So I'm all the more
astonished when I recall that lost fish rising,
leaving the water, and then returning.
The feeling of loss that gripped me then
grips me still. How can I communicate what I feel
about any of this? Inside, they go on
conversing in their own language.
            I decide to walk
alongside the river. It's the kind of night

that brings men and rivers close.
I go for a ways, then stop. Realizing
that I haven't been close. Not
in the longest time. There's been
this waiting that's gone along with me
wherever I go. But the hope widening now
that something will rise up and splash.
I want to hear it, and move on.

The Pen

The pen that told the truth
went into the washing machine
for its trouble. Came out
an hour later, and was tossed
in the dryer with jeans
and a western shirt. Days passed
while it lay quietly on the desk
under the window. Lay there
thinking it was finished.
Without a single conviction
to its name. It didn't have
the will to go on, even if it'd wanted.
But one morning, an hour or so
before sunrise, it came to life
and wrote:
"The damp fields asleep in moonlight."
Then it was still again.
Its usefulness in this life
clearly at an end.

He shook it and whacked it
on the desk. Then gave up
on it, or nearly.
Once more though, with the greatest
effort, it summoned its last
reserves. This is what it wrote:

"A light wind, and beyond the window
trees swimming in the golden morning air."

He tried to write some more
but that was all. The pen
quit working forever.
By and by it was put
into the stove along with
other junk. And much later
it was another pen,
an undistinguished pen
that hadn't proved itself
yet, that facilely wrote:
"Darkness gathers in the branches.
Stay inside. Keep still."

The Prize

He was never the same, they said, after that.
And they were right. He left home, glad for his life.
Fell under the spell of Italian opera.
A gout stool was built into the front of his sedan chair.
His family went on living in a hut without a chimney.
One season very much like another for them.
What did they know?
A river wound through their valley.
At night the candles flickered, blinking like eyelashes.
As though tobacco smoke burned their eyes.
But nobody smoked in that stinking place.
Nobody sang or wrote cantatas.
When he died it was they who had to identify the body.
It was terrible!
His friends couldn't remember him.
Not even what he'd looked like the day before.
His father spat and rode off to kill squirrels.
His sister cradled his head in her arms.
His mother wept and went through his pockets.
Nothing had changed.
He was back where he belonged.
As though he'd never left.
Easy enough to say he should have declined it.
But would you?

An Account

He began the poem at the kitchen table,
one leg crossed over the other.
He wrote for a time, as if
only half interested in the result. It wasn't
as if the world didn't have enough poems.
The world had plenty of poems. Besides,
he'd been away for months.
He hadn't even *read* a poem in months.
What kind of life was this? A life
where a man was too busy even to read poems?
No life at all. Then he looked out the window,
down the hill to Frank's house.
A nice house situated near the water.
He remembered Frank opening his door
every morning at nine o'clock.
Going out for his walks.
He drew nearer the table, and uncrossed his legs.

Last night he'd heard an account
of Frank's death from Ed, another neighbor.
A man the same age as Frank,
and Frank's good friend. Frank
and his wife watching TV. *Hill Street Blues.*
Frank's favorite show. When he gasps
twice, is thrown back in his chair—
"as if he'd been electrocuted." That fast,
he was dead. His color draining away.

He was grey, turning black. Betty runs
out of the house in her robe. Runs
to a neighbor's house where a girl knows
something about CPR. *She's* watching
the same show! They run back
to Frank's house. Frank totally black now,
in his chair in front of the TV.
The cops and other desperate characters
moving across the screen, raising their voices,
yelling at each other, while this neighbor girl
hauls Frank out of his chair onto the floor.
Tears open his shirt. Goes to work.
Frank being the first real-life victim
she's ever had.

                    She places her lips
on Frank's icy lips. A dead man's lips. Black lips.
And black his face and hands and arms.
Black too his chest where the shirt's been torn,
exposing the sparse hairs that grew there.
Long after she must've known better, she goes on
with it. Pressing her lips against his
unresponsive lips. Then stopping to beat on him
with clenched fists. Pressing her lips to his again,
and then again. Even after it's too late and it
was clear he wasn't coming back, she went on with it.
This girl, beating on him with her fists, calling
him every name she could think of. Weeping
when they took him away
from her. And someone thought to turn off
the images pulsing across the screen.

In the meadow this afternoon, I fetch
any number of crazy memories. That
undertaker asking my mother did she
want to buy the entire suit to bury my dad in,
or just the coat? I don't
have to provide the answer to this,
or anything else. But, hey, he went
into the furnace wearing his britches.

This morning I looked at his picture.
Big, heavyset guy in the last year
of his life. Holding a monster salmon
in front of the shack where he lived
in Fortuna, California. My dad.
He's nothing now. Reduced to a cup of ashes,
and some tiny bones. No way
is this any way
to end your life as a man.
Though as Hemingway correctly pointed out,
all stories, if continued far enough,
end in death. Truly.

Lord, it's almost fall.
A flock of Canada geese passes
high overhead. The little mare lifts
her head, shivers once, goes back
to grazing. I think I will lie down

in this sweet grass. I'll shut my eyes
and listen to wind, and the sound of wings.
Just dream for an hour, glad to be here
and not there. There's that. But also
the terrible understanding
that men I loved have left
for some other, lesser place.

Loafing

I looked into the room a moment ago,
and this is what I saw—
my chair in its place by the window,
the book turned facedown on the table.
And on the sill, the cigarette
left burning in its ashtray.
Malingerer! my uncle yelled at me
so long ago. He was right.
I've set aside time today,
same as every day,
for doing nothing at all.

Sinew

The girl minding the store.
She stands at the window
picking a piece of pork
from her teeth. Idly
watching the men in serge suits,
waistcoats, and ties,
dapping for trout on Lough Gill,
near the Isle of Innisfree.
The remains of her midday meal
congealing on the sill.
The air is still and warm.
A cuckoo calls.

Close in, a man in a boat,
wearing a hat, looks
toward shore, the little store,
and the girl. He looks, whips
his line, and looks some more.
She leans closer to the glass.
Goes out then to the lakeside.
But it's the cuckoo in the bush
that has her attention.

The man strikes a fish,
all business now.
The girl goes on working
at the sinew in her teeth.

But she watches this well-dressed
man reaching out
to slip a net under his fish.

In a minute, shyly, he floats near.
Holds up his catch for the girl's pleasure.
Doffs his hat. She stirs and smiles
a little. Raises her hand.
A gesture which starts the bird
in flight, toward Innisfree.

The man casts and casts again.
His line cuts the air. His fly
touches the water, and waits.
But what does this man
really care for trout?
What he'll take
from this day is the memory of
a girl working her finger
inside her mouth as their glances
meet, and a bird flies up.

They look at each other and smile.
In the still afternoon.
With not a word lost between them.

Waiting

Left off the highway and
down the hill. At the
bottom, hang another left.
Keep bearing left. The road
will make a Y. Left again.
There's a creek on the left.
Keep going. Just before
the road ends, there'll be
another road. Take it
and no other. Otherwise,
your life will be ruined
forever. There's a log house
with a shake roof, on the left.
It's not that house. It's
the next house, just over
a rise. The house
where trees are laden with
fruit. Where phlox, forsythia,
and marigold grow. It's
the house where the woman
stands in the doorway
wearing sun in her hair. The one
who's been waiting
all this time.
The woman who loves you.
The one who can say,
"What's kept you?"

FOUR

The Debate

This morning I'm torn
between responsibility to
myself, duty
to my publisher, and the pull
I feel toward the river
below my house. The winter-
run steelhead are in,
is the problem. It's
nearly dawn, the tide
is high. Even as
this little dilemma
occurs, and the debate
goes on, fish
are starting into the river.
Hey, I'll live, and be happy,
whatever I decide.

Its Course

The man who took 38 steelhead out
of this little river
last winter (his name is Bill Zitter,
"last name in the directory")
told me the river's changed its course
dramatically, he would even say
radically, since he first moved here,
he and his wife. It used to flow
"yonder, where those houses are."
When salmon crossed that shoal at night,
they made a noise like water boiling
in a cauldron, a noise like you were
scrubbing something on a washboard.
"It could wake you up from a deep sleep."
Now, there's no more salmon run.
And he won't fish for steelhead
this winter, because Mrs. Zitter's
eaten up with cancer. He's needed
at home. The doctors expect
she'll pass away before the New Year.

"Right where you're living," he goes on,
"that used to be a motorcycle run.
They'd come from all over the county
to race their bikes. They'd tear up
that hill and then go down
the other side. But they were

just having fun. Young guys. Not
like those gangs today, those bad apples."
I wished him luck. Shook his hand.
And went home to my house, the place
they used to race motorcycles.

Later, at the table in my room, looking
out over the water, I give some thought
to just what it is I'm doing here.
What it is I'm after in this life.
It doesn't seem like much,
in the end. I remembered what he'd said
about the young men
and their motorcycles.
Those young men who must be old men
now. Zitter's age, or else
my age. Old enough, in either case.
And for a moment I imagine
the roar of the engines as they surge
up this hill, the laughter and
shouting as they spill, swear, get up,
shake themselves off, and walk
their bikes to the top.
Where they slap each other on the back
and reach in the burlap bag for a beer.
Now and then one of them gunning it
for all it's worth, forcing his way
to the top, and then going lickety-
split down the other side!
Disappearing in a roar, in a cloud of dust.
Right outside my window is where
all this happened. We vanish soon enough.
Soon enough, eaten up.

September

September, and somewhere the last
of the sycamore leaves
have returned to earth.

Wind clears the sky of clouds.

What's left here? Grouse, silver salmon,
and the struck pine not far from the house.
A tree hit by lightning. But even now
beginning to live again. A few shoots
miraculously appearing.

Stephen Foster's "Maggie by My Side"
plays on the radio.

I listen with my eyes far away.

The White Field

Woke up feeling anxious and bone-lonely.
Unable to give my attention to anything
beyond coffee and cigarettes. Of course,
the best antidote for this is work.
"What is your duty? What each day requires,"
said Goethe, or someone like him.
But I didn't have any sense of duty.
I didn't feel like doing anything.
I felt as if I'd lost my will, and my memory.
And I had. If someone had come along
at that minute, as I was slurping coffee, and said,
"Where were you when I needed you?
How have you spent your life? What'd you do
even two days ago?" What could I have said?
I'd only have gawped. Then I tried.
Remembered back a couple of days.
Driving to the end of that road with Morris.
Taking our fishing gear from the jeep.
Strapping on snowshoes, and walking across the white field
toward the river. Every so often
turning around to look at the strange tracks
we'd left. Feeling glad enough to be alive
as we kicked up rabbits, and ducks passed over.

Then to come upon Indians standing in the river
in chest-high waders! Dragging a net for steelhead
through the pool we planned to fish.

The hole just above the river's mouth.
Them working in relentless silence. Cigarettes
hanging from their lips. Not once
looking up or otherwise acknowledging
our existence.

"Christ almighty," Morris said.
"This is for the birds." And we snowshoed back
across the field, cursing our luck, cursing Indians.
The day in all other respects unremarkable.
Except when I was driving the jeep
and Morris showed me the three-inch scar
across the back of his hand from the hot stove
he'd fallen against in elk camp.

But this happened the day before yesterday.
It's yesterday that got away, that slipped through
the net and back to sea.

Yet hearing those distant voices down the road just now,
I seem to recall everything. And I understand
that yesterday had its own relentless logic.
Just like today, and all the other days in my life.

Shooting

I wade through wheat up to my belly,
cradling a shotgun in my arms.
Tess is asleep back at the ranch house.
The moon pales. Then loses face completely
as the sun spears up over the mountains.

Why do I pick this moment
to remember my aunt taking me aside that time
and saying, *What I am going to tell you now
you will remember every day of your life?*
But that's all I can remember.

I've never been able to trust memory. My own
or anyone else's. I'd like to know what on earth
I'm doing here in this strange regalia.
It's my friend's wheat—this much is true.
And right now, his dog is on point.

Tess is opposed to killing for sport,
or any other reason. Yet not long ago she
threatened to kill me. The dog inches forward.
I stop moving. I can't see or hear
my breath any longer.

Step by tiny step, the day advances. Suddenly,
the air explodes with birds.

Tess sleeps through it. When she wakes,
October will be over. Guns and talk
of shooting behind us.

The Window

A storm blew in last night and knocked out
the electricity. When I looked
through the window, the trees were translucent.
Bent and covered with rime. A vast calm
lay over the countryside.
I knew better. But at that moment
I felt I'd never in my life made any
false promises, nor committed
so much as one indecent act. My thoughts
were virtuous. Later on that morning,
of course, electricity was restored.
The sun moved from behind the clouds,
melting the hoarfrost.
And things stood as they had before.

Heels

Begin nude, looking for the socks
worn yesterday and maybe
the day before, etc. They're not
on your feet, but they can't
have gone far. They're under the bed!
You take them up and give them
a good shaking to free the dust.
Shaking's no more than they deserve.
Now run your hand down the limp,
shapeless things. These blue,
brown, black, green, or grey socks.
You feel you could put your arm into one
and it wouldn't make a particle
of difference. So why not do this
one thing you're inclined to do?
You draw them on over your fingers
and work them up to the elbow.
You close and open your fists. Then
close them again, and keep them that way.
Now your hands are like heels
that could stamp
on things. Anything.
You're heading for the door
when a draft of air hits your ankles
and you're reminded of those wild swans
at Coole, and the wild swans at places
you've never heard of; let alone

visited. You understand now
just how far away you are from all that
as you fumble with the closed door.
Then the door opens! You wanted it
to be morning, as expected
after a night's uneasy sleep.
But stars are overhead, and the moon
reels above dark trees.
You raise your arms and gesture.
A man with socks over his hands
under the night sky.
It's like, but not like, a dream.

The Phone Booth

She slumps in the booth, weeping
into the phone. Asking a question
or two, and weeping some more.
Her companion, an old fellow in jeans
and denim shirt, stands waiting
his turn to talk, and weep.
She hands him the phone.
For a minute they are together
in the tiny booth, his tears
dropping alongside hers. Then
she goes to lean against the fender
of their sedan. And listens
to him talk about arrangements.

I watch all this from my car.
I don't have a phone at home, either.
I sit behind the wheel,
smoking, waiting to make
my own arrangements. Pretty soon
he hangs up. Comes out and wipes his face.
They get in the car and sit
with the windows rolled up.
The glass grows steamy as she
leans into him, as he puts
his arm around her shoulders.
The workings of comfort in that cramped, public place.

I take my small change over
to the booth, and step inside.
But leaving the door open, it's
so close in there. The phone still warm to the touch.
I hate to use a phone
that's just brought news of death.
But I have to, it being the only phone
for miles, and one that might
listen without taking sides.

I put in coins and wait.
Those people in the car wait too.
He starts the engine then kills it.
Where to? None of us able
to figure it. Not knowing
where the next blow might fall,
or why. The ringing at the other end
stops when she picks it up.
Before I can say two words, the phone
begins to shout, "I told you it's over!
Finished! You can go
to hell as far as I'm concerned!"

I drop the phone and pass my hand
across my face. I close and open the door.
The couple in the sedan roll
their windows down and
watch, their tears stilled
for a moment in the face of this distraction.
Then they roll their windows up
and sit behind the glass. We
don't go anywhere for a while.
And then we go.

New snow onto old ice last night. Now,
errand-bound to town, preoccupied with the mudge
in his head, he applied his brakes too fast.
And found himself in a big car out of control,
moving broadside down the road in the immense
stillness of the winter morning. Headed
inexorably for the intersection.
The things that were passing through his mind?
The news film on TV of three alley cats
and a rhesus monkey with electrodes implanted
in their skulls; the time he stopped to photograph
a buffalo near where the Little Big Horn
joined the Big Horn; his new graphite rod
with the Limited Lifetime Warranty;
the polyps the doctor'd found on his bowel;
the Bukowski line that flew
through his mind from time to time:
We'd all like to pass by in a 1995 Cadillac.
His head a hive of arcane activity.
Even during the time it took his car
to slide around on the highway and point him
back in the direction he'd come from.
The direction of home, and relative security.
The engine was dead. The immense stillness
descended once more. He took off his woolen cap
and wiped his forehead. But after a moment's
consideration, started his car, turned around

and continued on into town.
More carefully, yes. But thinking all the while
along the same lines as before. Old ice, new snow.
Cats. A monkey. Fishing. Wild buffalo.
The sheer poetry in musing on Cadillacs
that haven't been built yet. The chastening effect
of the doctor's fingers.

Simple

A break in the clouds. The blue
outline of the mountains.
Dark yellow of the fields.
Black river. What am I doing here,
lonely and filled with remorse?

I go on casually eating from the bowl
of raspberries. If I were dead,
I remind myself, I wouldn't
be eating them. It's not so simple.
It is that simple.

The Scratch

I woke up with a spot of blood
over my eye. A scratch
halfway across my forehead. But
I'm sleeping alone these days.
Why on earth would a man raise his hand
against himself, even in sleep?
It's this and similar questions
I'm trying to answer this morning.
As I study my face in the window.

Mother

My mother calls to wish me a Merry Christmas.
And to tell me if this snow keeps on
she intends to kill herself. I want to say
I'm not myself this morning, please
give me a break. I may have to borrow a psychiatrist
again. The one who always asks me the most fertile
of questions, "But what are you *really* feeling?"
Instead, I tell her one of our skylights
has a leak. While I'm talking, the snow is
melting onto the couch. I say I've switched to All-Bran
so there's no need to worry any longer
about me getting cancer, and her money coming to an end.
She hears me out. Then informs me
she's leaving *this goddamn place*. Somehow. The only time
she wants to see it, or me again, is from her coffin.
Suddenly, I ask if she remembers the time Dad
was dead drunk and bobbed the tail of the Labrador pup.
I go on like this for a while, talking about
those days. She listens, waiting her turn.
It continues to snow. It snows and snows
as I hang on the phone. The trees and rooftops
are covered with it. How can I talk about this?
How can I possibly explain what I'm feeling?

The Child

Seeing the child again.
Not having seen him
for six months. His face
seems broader than last time.
Heavier. Almost coarse.
More like his father's now.
Devoid of mirth. The eyes
narrowed and without
expression. Don't expect
gentleness or pity
from this child, now or ever.
There's something rough,
even cruel, in the grasp
of his small hand.
I turn him loose.
His shoes scuff against
each other as he makes for the door.
As it opens. As he give his cry.

The Fields

I was nearsighted and had to get up close
so I could see it in the first place: the earth
that'd been torn with a disk or plow.
But I could smell it, and I didn't like it.
To me it was gruesome, suggesting death
and the grave. I was running once and fell
and came up with a mouthful. That
was enough to make me want to keep my distance
from fields just after they'd been sliced open
to expose whatever lay teeming underneath.
And I never cared anything for gardens, either.
Those over-ripe flowers in summer bloom.
Or spuds lying just under the surface
with only part of their faces showing.
Those places I shied away from, too. Even today
I can do without a garden. But something's changed.

There's nothing I like better now than to walk into
a freshly turned field and kneel and let the soft dirt
slide through my fingers. I'm lucky to live
close to the fields I'm talking about.
I've even made friends with some of the farmers.
The same men who used to strike me
as unfriendly and sinister.
So what if the worms come sooner or later?
And what's it matter if the winter snow piles up

higher than fences, then melts and drains away
deep into the earth to water what's left of us?
It's okay. Quite a lot was accomplished here, after all.
I gambled and lost, sure. Then gambled some more,
and won. My eyesight is failing. But if I move
up close and look carefully, I can see all kinds of life
in the earth. Not just worms, but beetles, ants, ladybugs.
Things like that. I'm gladdened, not concerned with
   the sight.
It's nice to walk out into a field any day
that I want and not feel afraid. I love to reach
down and bring a handful of dirt right up under my nose.
And I can push with my feet and feel the earth give
under my shoes. I can stand there quietly
under the great balanced sky, motionless.
With this impulse to take off my shoes.
But just an impulse. More important,
this not moving. And then
Amazing! to walk that opened field—
and keep walking.

After Reading Two Towns in Provence

for M.F.K. Fisher

I went out for a minute and
left your book on the table.
Something came up. Next morning,
at a quarter to six,
dawn began. Men had already
gone into the fields to work.
Windrows of leaves lay
alongside the track.
Reminding me of fall.
I turned to the first page
and began to read.

I spent the entire morning
in your company, in Aix,
in the South of France.
When I looked up,
it was twelve o'clock.

And they all said I'd never find a place
for myself in this life!
Said I'd never be happy,
not in this world, or the next.
That's how much they knew.
Those dopes.

Evening

I fished alone that languid autumn evening.
Fished as darkness kept coming on.
Experiencing exceptional loss and then
exceptional joy when I brought a silver salmon
to the boat, and dipped a net under the fish.
Secret heart! When I looked into the moving water
and up at the dark outline of the mountains
behind the town, nothing hinted then
I would suffer so this longing
to be back once more, before I die.
Far from everything, and far from myself.

The Rest

Clouds hang loosely over this mountain range
behind my house. In a while, the light
will go and the wind come up
to scatter these clouds, or some others,
across the sky.
                    I drop to my knees,
roll the big salmon onto its side
on the wet grass, and begin to use
the knife I was born with. Soon
I'll be at the table in the living room,
trying to raise the dead. The moon
and the dark water my companions.
My hands are silvery with scales.
Fingers mingling with the dark blood.
Finally, I cut loose the massive head.
I bury what needs burying
and keep the rest. Take one last look
at the high blue light. Turn
toward my house. My night.

Slippers

The four of us sitting around that afternoon.
Caroline telling her dream. How she woke up
barking this one night. And found her little dog,
Teddy, beside the bed, watching.
The man who was her husband at the time
watched too as she told of the dream.
Listened carefully. Even smiled. But
there was something in his eyes. A way
of looking, and a look. We've all had it . . .
Already he was in love with a woman
named Jane, though this is no judgment
on him, or Jane, or anyone else. Everyone went on
to tell a dream. I didn't have any.
I looked at your feet, tucked up on the sofa,
in slippers. All I could think to say,
but didn't, was how those slippers were still warm
one night when I picked them up
where you'd left them. I put them beside the bed.
But a quilt fell and covered them
during the night. Next morning, you looked
everywhere for them. Then called downstairs,
"I found my slippers!" This is a small thing,
I know, and between us. Nevertheless,
it has moment. Those lost slippers. And
that cry of delight.
It's okay that this happened

a year or more ago. It could've been
yesterday, or the day before. What difference?
Delight, and a cry.

Asia

It's good to live near the water.
Ships pass so close to land
a man could reach out
and break a branch from one of the willow trees
that grow here. Horses run wild
down by the water, along the beach.
If the men on board wanted, they could
fashion a lariat and throw it
and bring one of the horses on deck.
Something to keep them company
for the long journey East.

From my balcony I can read the faces
of the men as they stare at the horses,
the trees, and two-story houses.
I know what they're thinking
when they see a man waving from a balcony,
his red car in the drive below.
They look at him and consider themselves
lucky. What a mysterious piece
of good fortune, they think, that's brought
them all this way to the deck of a ship
bound for Asia. Those years of doing odd jobs,
or working in warehouses, or longshoring,
or simply hanging out on the docks,
are forgotten about. Those things happened

to other, younger men,
if they happened at all.

                The men on board
raise their arms and wave back.
Then stand still, gripping the rail,
as the ship glides past. The horses
move from under the trees and into the sun.
They stand like statues of horses.
Watching the ship as it passes.
Waves breaking against the ship.
Against the beach. And in the mind
of the horses, where
it is always Asia.

The Gift

for Tess

Snow began falling late last night. Wet flakes
dropping past windows, snow covering
the skylights. We watched for a time, surprised
and happy. Glad to be here, and nowhere else.
I loaded up the wood stove. Adjusted the flue.
We went to bed, where I closed my eyes at once.
But for some reason, before falling asleep,
I recalled the scene at the airport
in Buenos Aires the evening we left.
How still and deserted the place seemed!
Dead quiet except the sound of our engines
as we backed away from the gate and
taxied slowly down the runway in a light snow.
The windows in the terminal building dark.
No one in evidence, not even a ground crew. "It's as if
the whole place is in mourning," you said.

I opened my eyes. Your breathing said
you were fast asleep. I covered you with an arm
and went on from Argentina to recall a place
I lived in once in Palo Alto. No snow in Palo Alto.
But I had a room and two windows looking onto the
    Bayshore Freeway.
The refrigerator stood next to the bed.
When I became dehydrated in the middle of the night,
all I had to do to slake that thirst was reach out
and open the door. The light inside showed the way

to a bottle of cold water. A hot plate
sat in the bathroom close to the sink.
When I shaved, the pan of water bubbled
on the coil next to the jar of coffee granules.

I sat on the bed one morning, dressed, clean-shaven,
drinking coffee, putting off what I'd decided to do. Finally
dialed Jim Houston's number in Santa Cruz.
And asked for 75 dollars. He said he didn't have it.
His wife had gone to Mexico for a week.
He simply didn't have it. He was coming up short
this month. "It's okay," I said. "I understand."
And I did. We talked a little
more, then hung up. He didn't have it.
I finished the coffee, more or less, just as the plane
lifted off the runway into the sunset.
I turned in the seat for one last look
at the lights of Buenos Aires. Then closed my eyes
for the long trip back.

This morning there's snow everywhere. We remark on it.
You tell me you didn't sleep well. I say
I didn't either. You had a terrible night. "Me too."
We're extraordinarily calm and tender with each other
as if sensing the other's rickety state of mind.
As if we knew what the other was feeling. We don't,
of course. We never do. No matter.
It's the tenderness I care about. That's the gift
this morning that moves and holds me.
Same as every morning.

ABOUT THE AUTHOR

RAYMOND CARVER was born in Clatskanie, Oregon, in 1939, and lived in Port Angeles, Washington, until his death on August 2, 1988. He was a Guggenheim Fellow in 1979 and was twice awarded grants from the National Endowment for the Arts. In 1983 Carver received the prestigious Mildred and Harold Strauss Living Award, and in 1985 *Poetry* magazine's Levinson Prize. In 1988 he was elected to the American Academy and Institute of Arts and Letters and was awarded a Doctorate of Letters from Hartford University. He received a Brandeis Citation for fiction in 1988. His work has been translated into more than twenty languages.